Weitao Yang's Paintings Work

A Moonlit Night on the Spring River

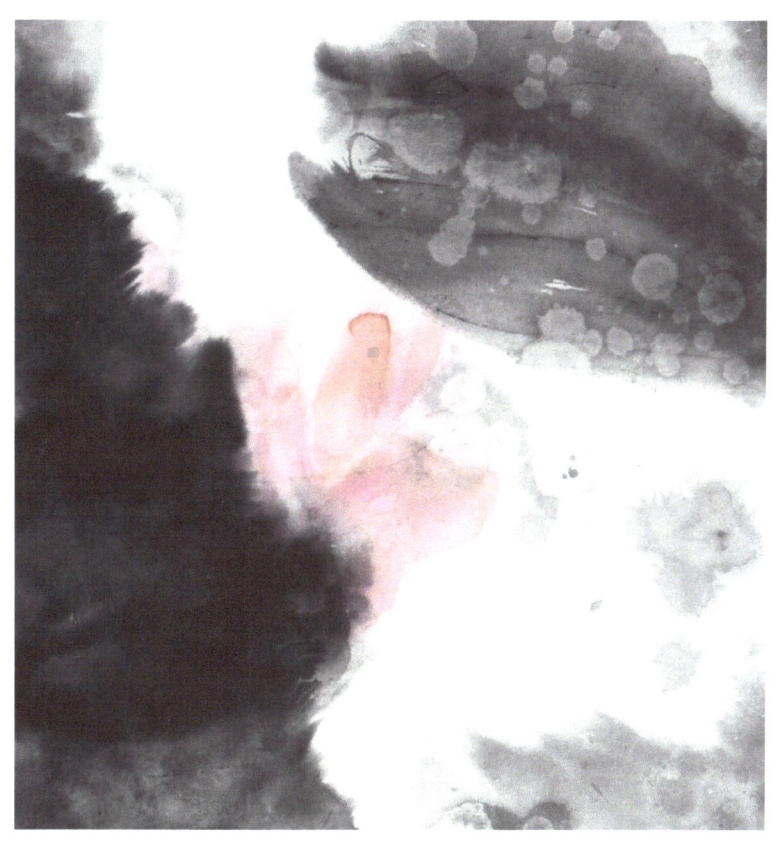

ABOUT THE AUTHOR
ARTIST YANG WEITAO

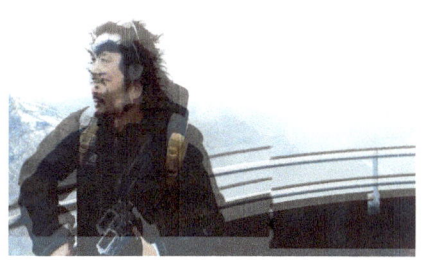

Yang Weitao
Pen name: Yang Dan, additional signature: Yijizhai.
Graduated from the Central Academy of Art and Design.
Member of Chinese Artists Association.
Member of Jiang Zhaohe Art Research Association of China Artists Association.
Now lives in Mountain lakes, New Jersey, USA.
His works have participated in the National Art Exhibition dozens of times and have won numerous awards.
Published personal work collections: "The Gate of the Master-Yang Weitao Modern Ink Figure Painting Collection", "Yang Weitao Ink Figure Painting Collection", "The Four Seasons of Ink-Yang Weitao Chinese Painting Works", "Yang Weitao Collection", "The Dream Is Also Gentle-Yang Weitao Illustration Works Collection" and more than 20 kinds.
China Central Television's calligraphy and painting channel filmed a feature film for it: "The Spiritual Journey of Yang Weitao"
The Chinese painting capital frequently shoots a disco for this: "Yang Weitao's Biography".
The above videos: Youtube and Tencent videos can be searched and watched.
Yang Weitao contact information:
Contact number: 1 201 754 3877
Email: wty4039@gmail.com

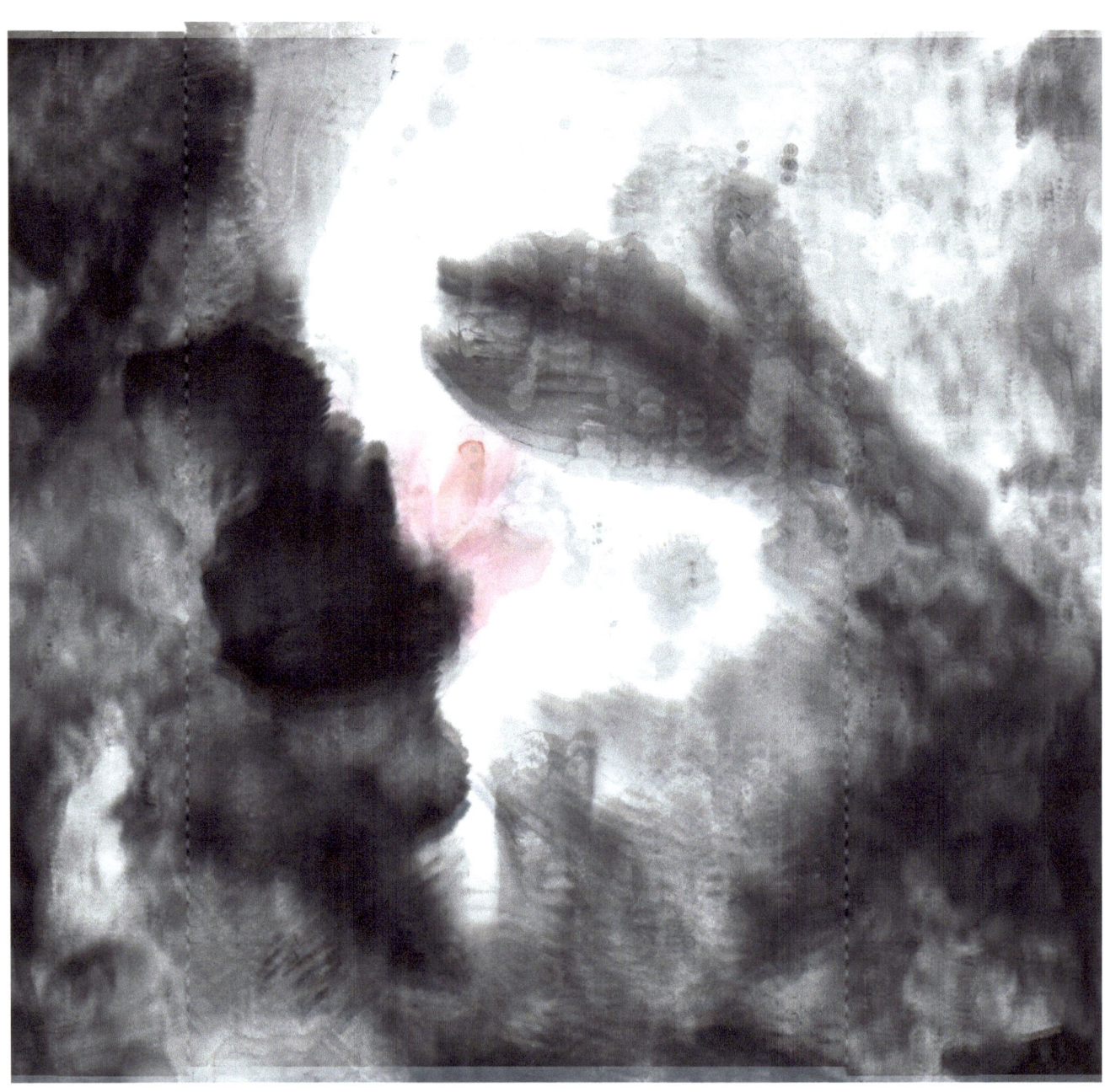

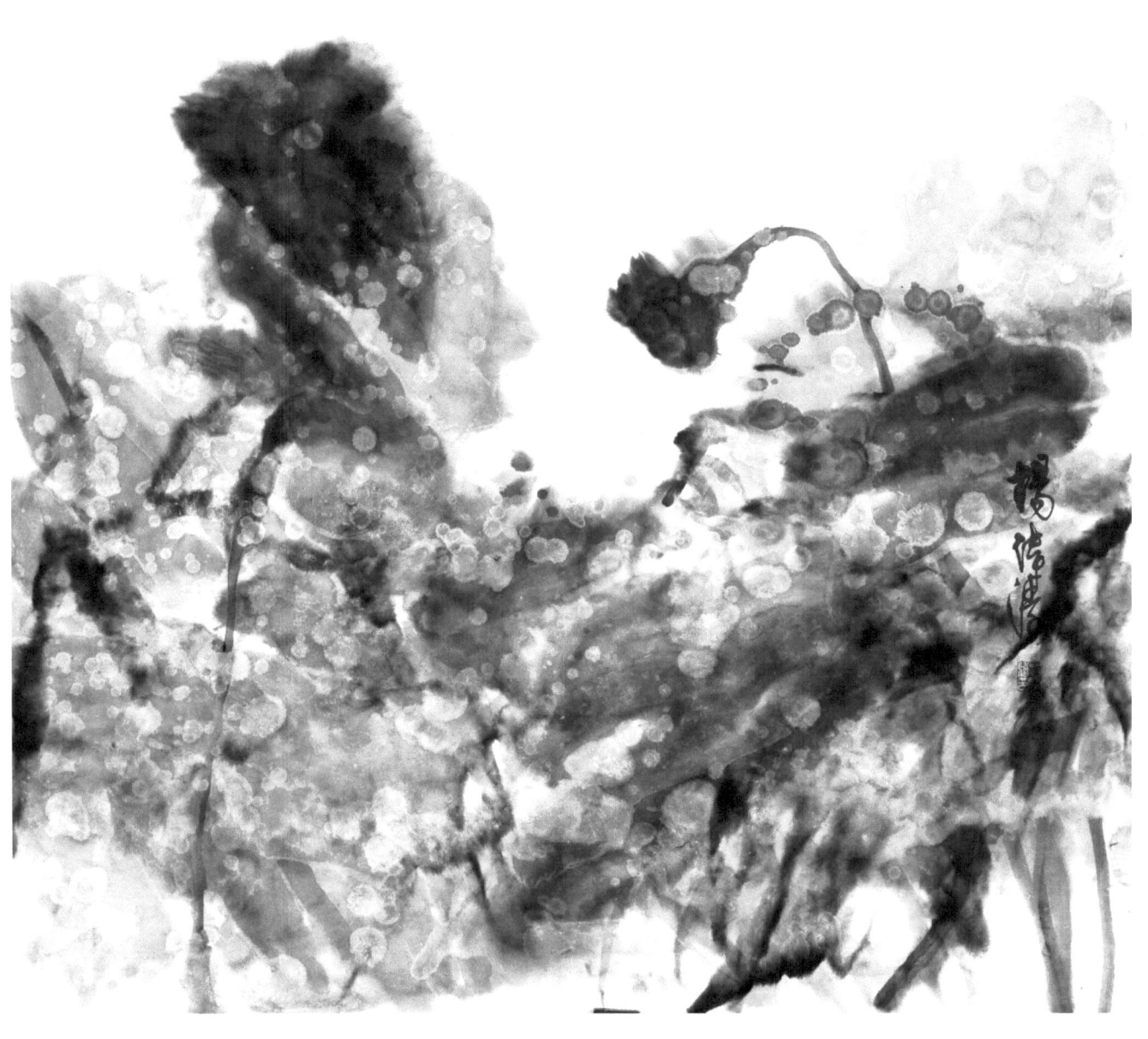

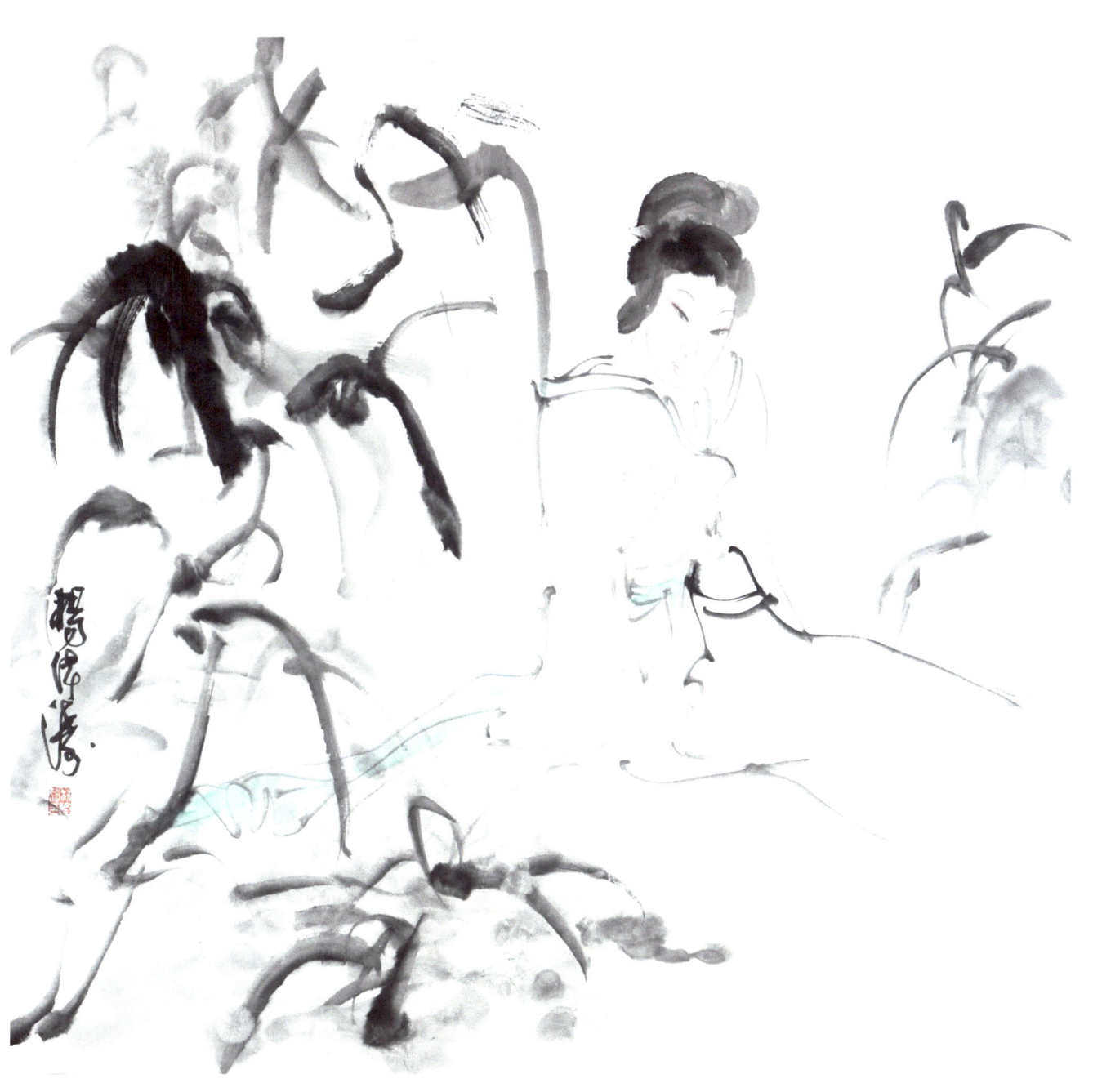

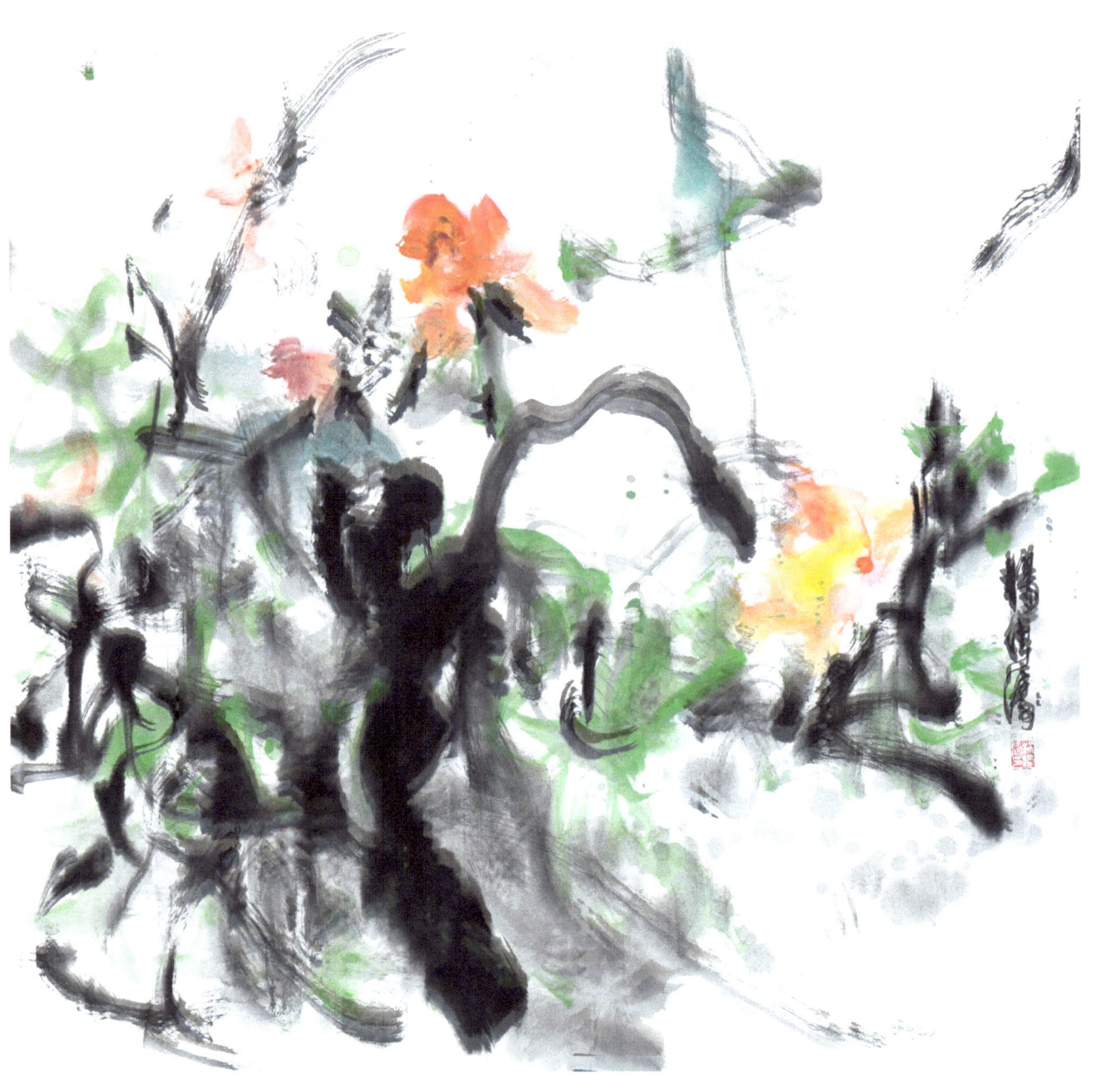

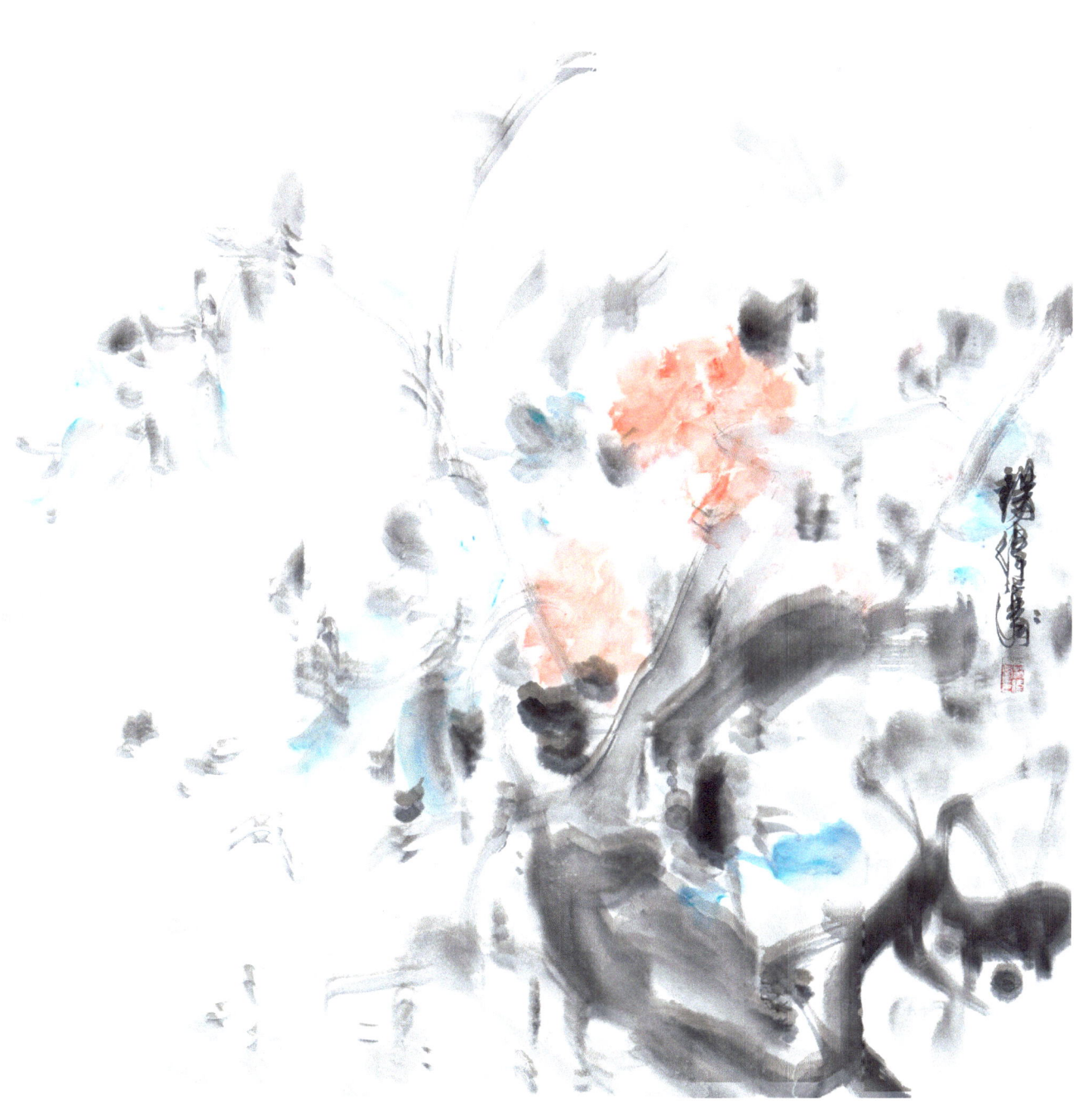

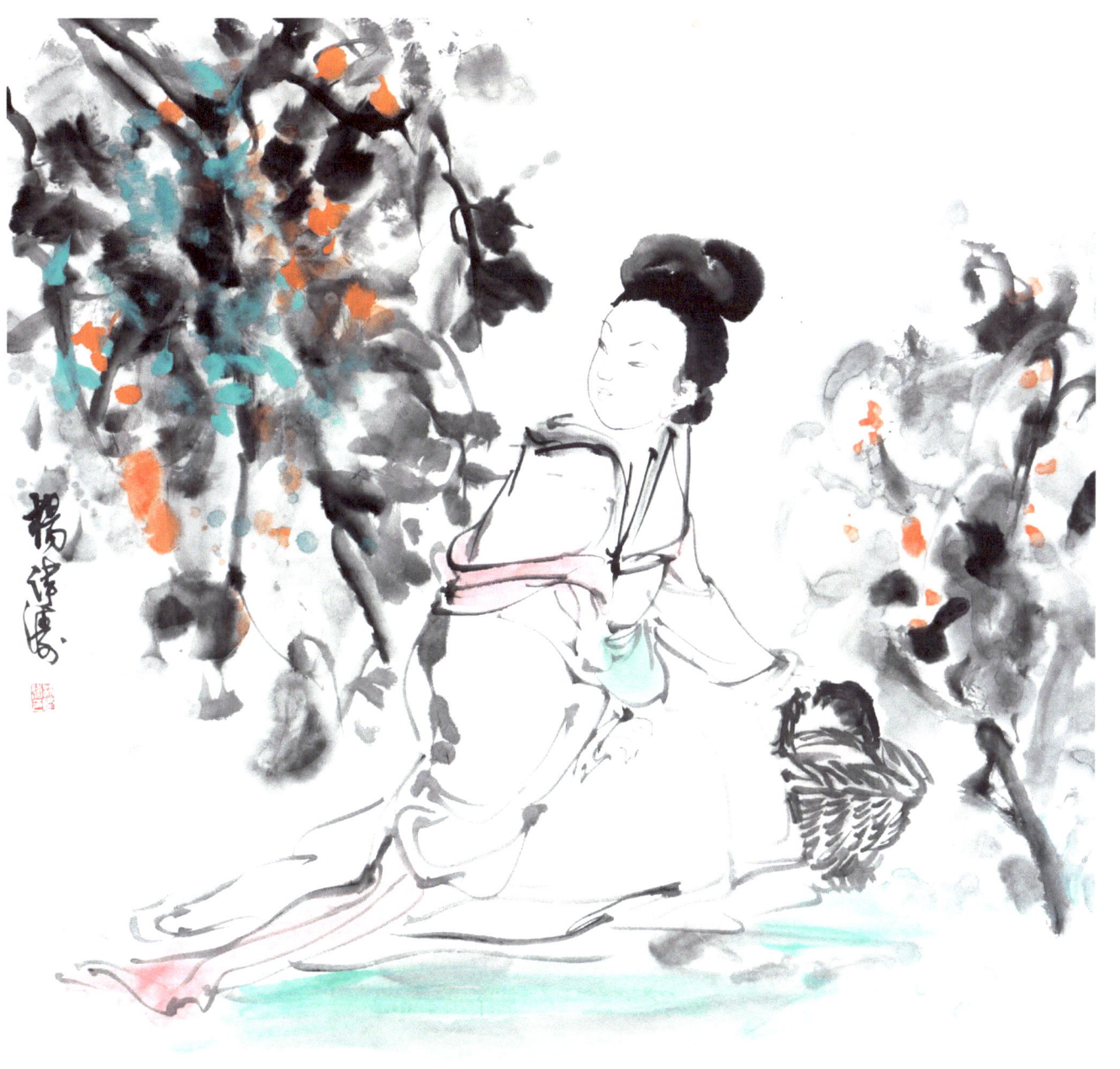

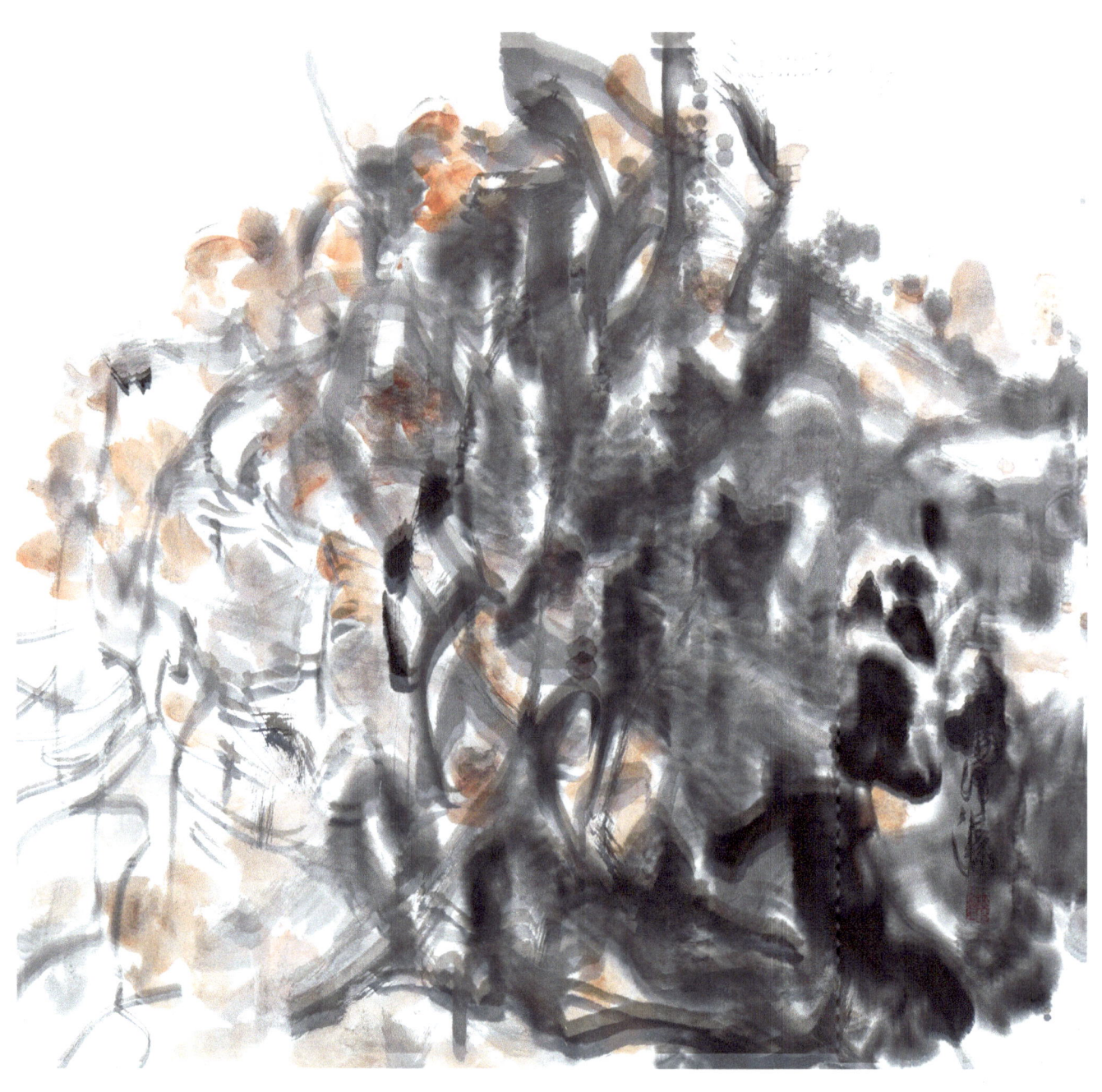

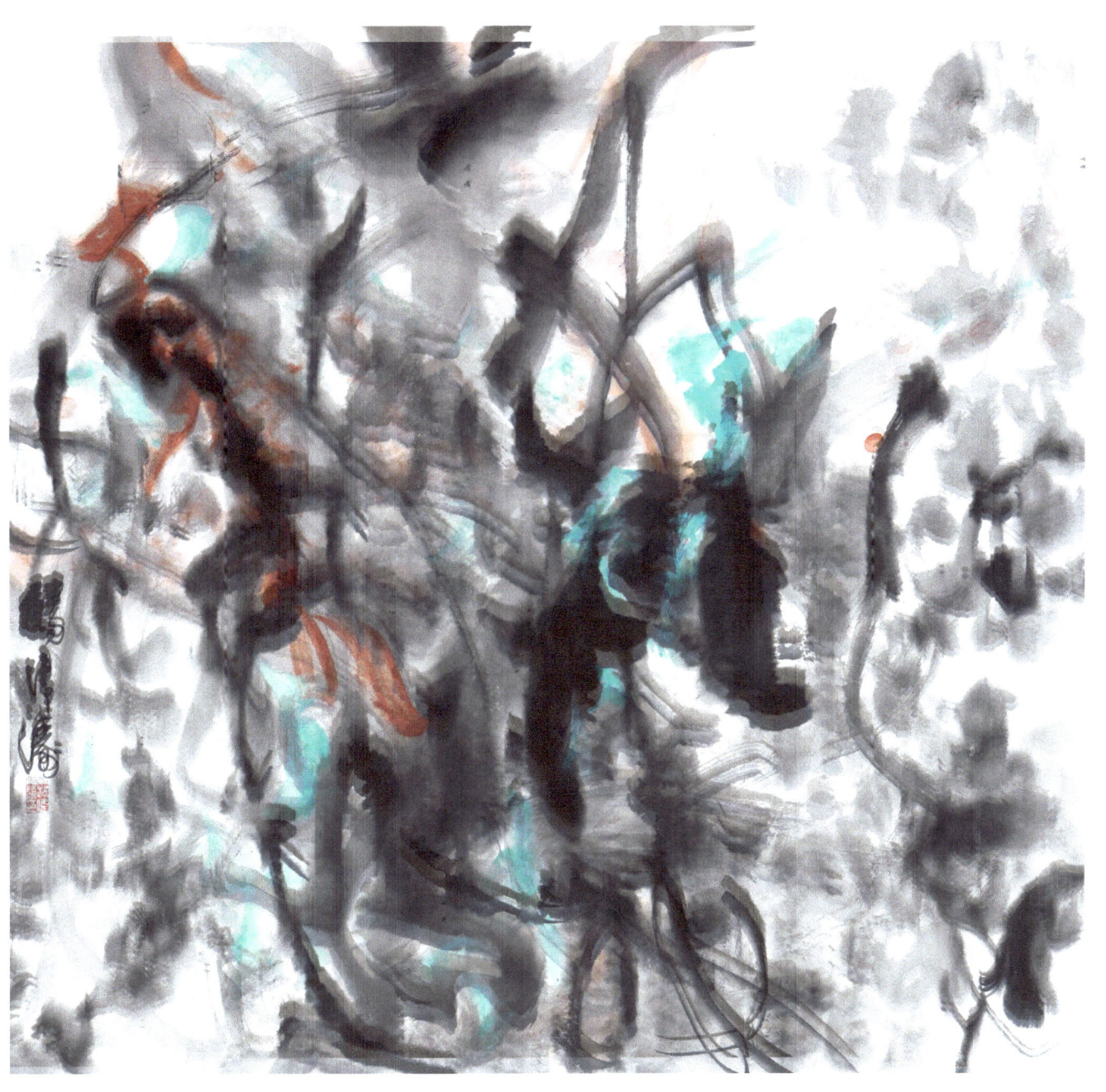

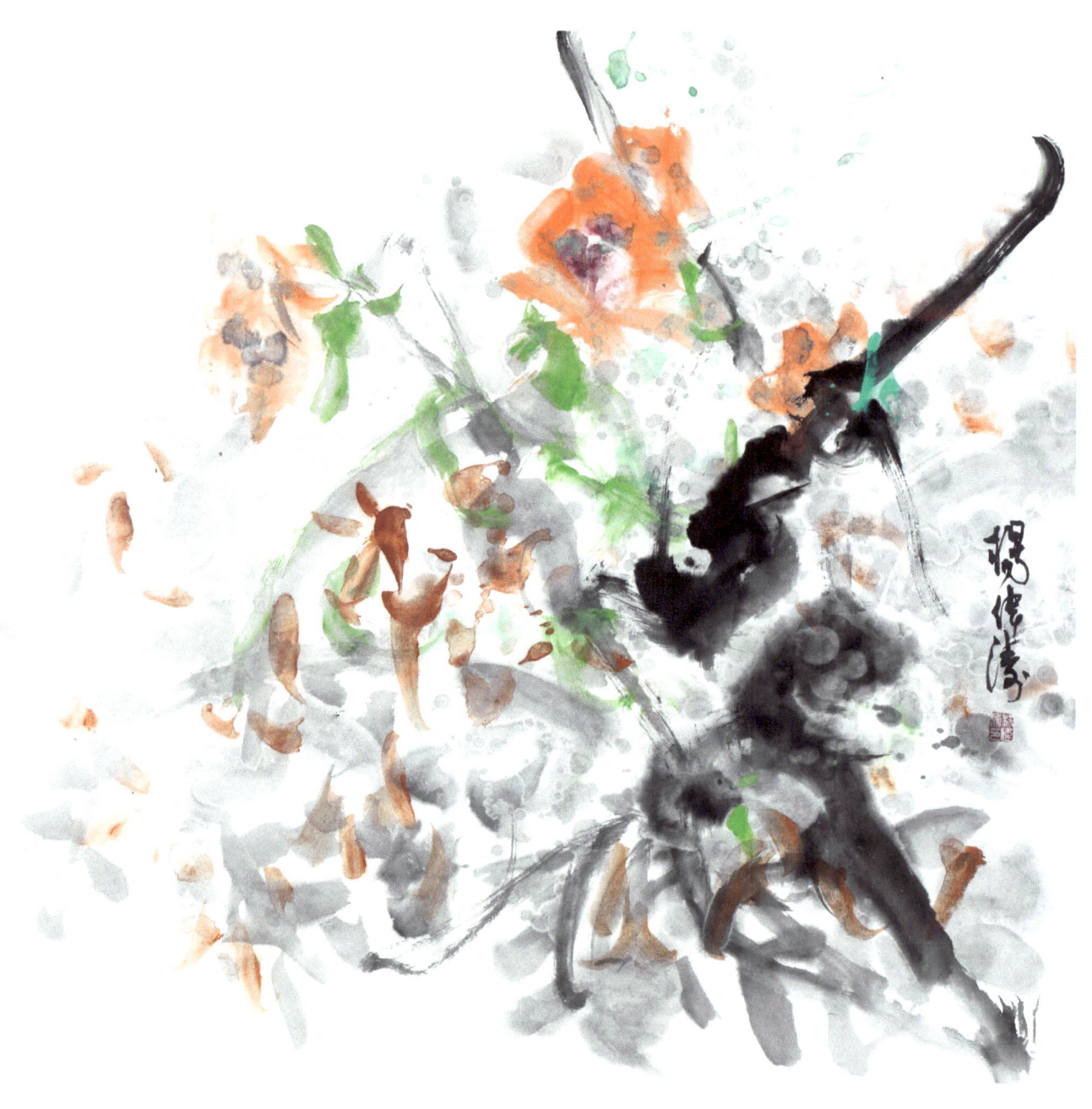

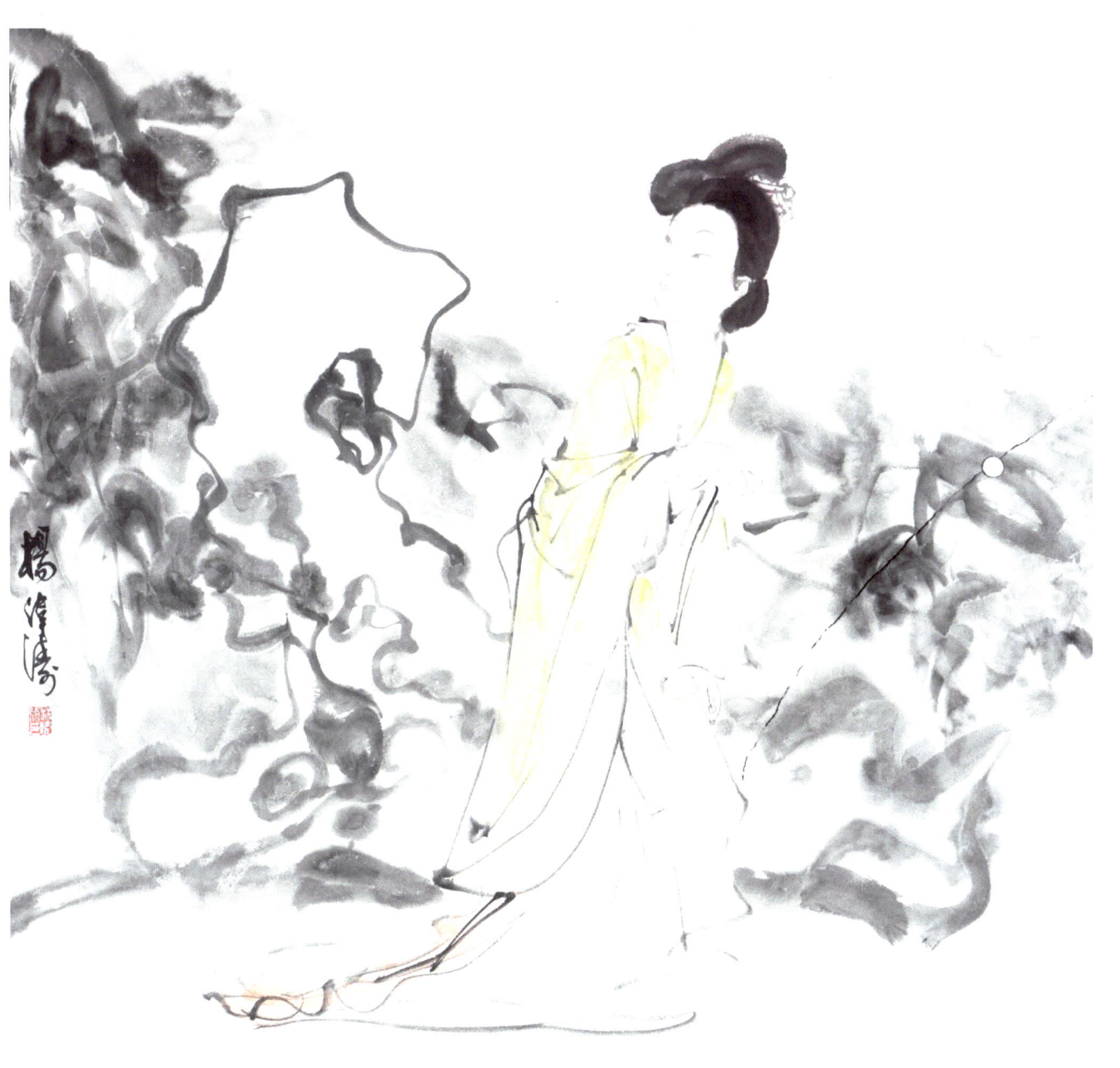

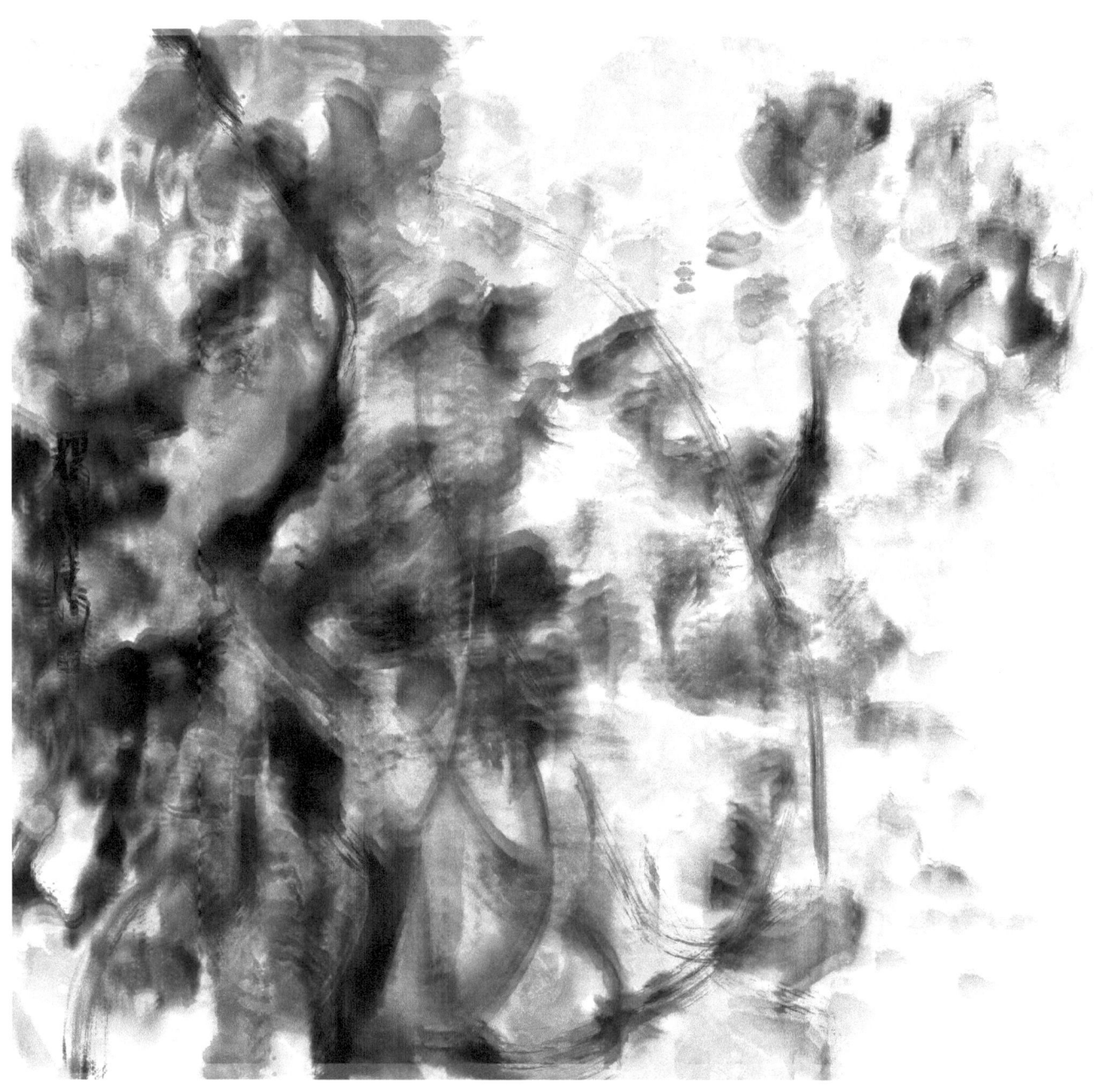

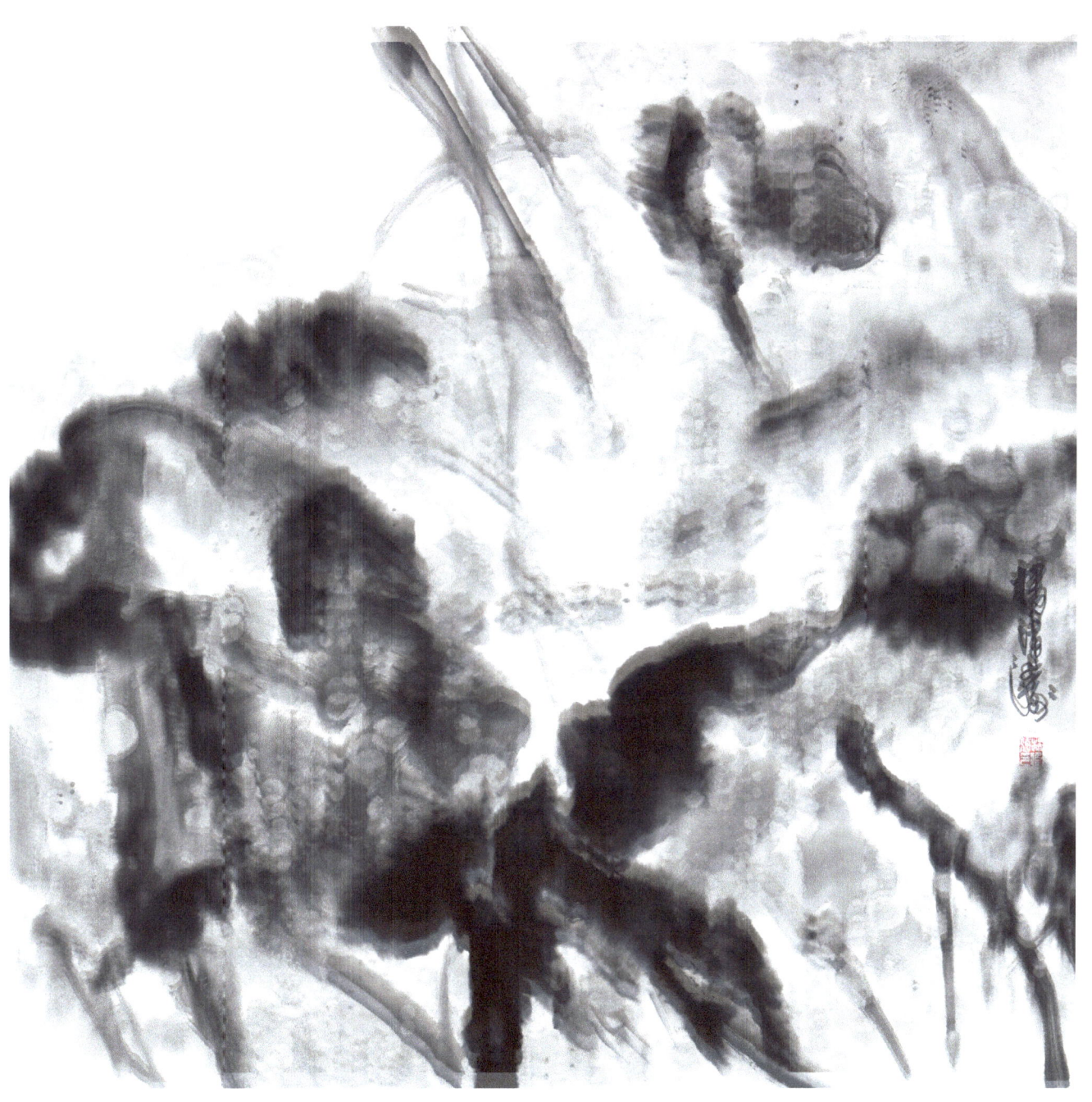

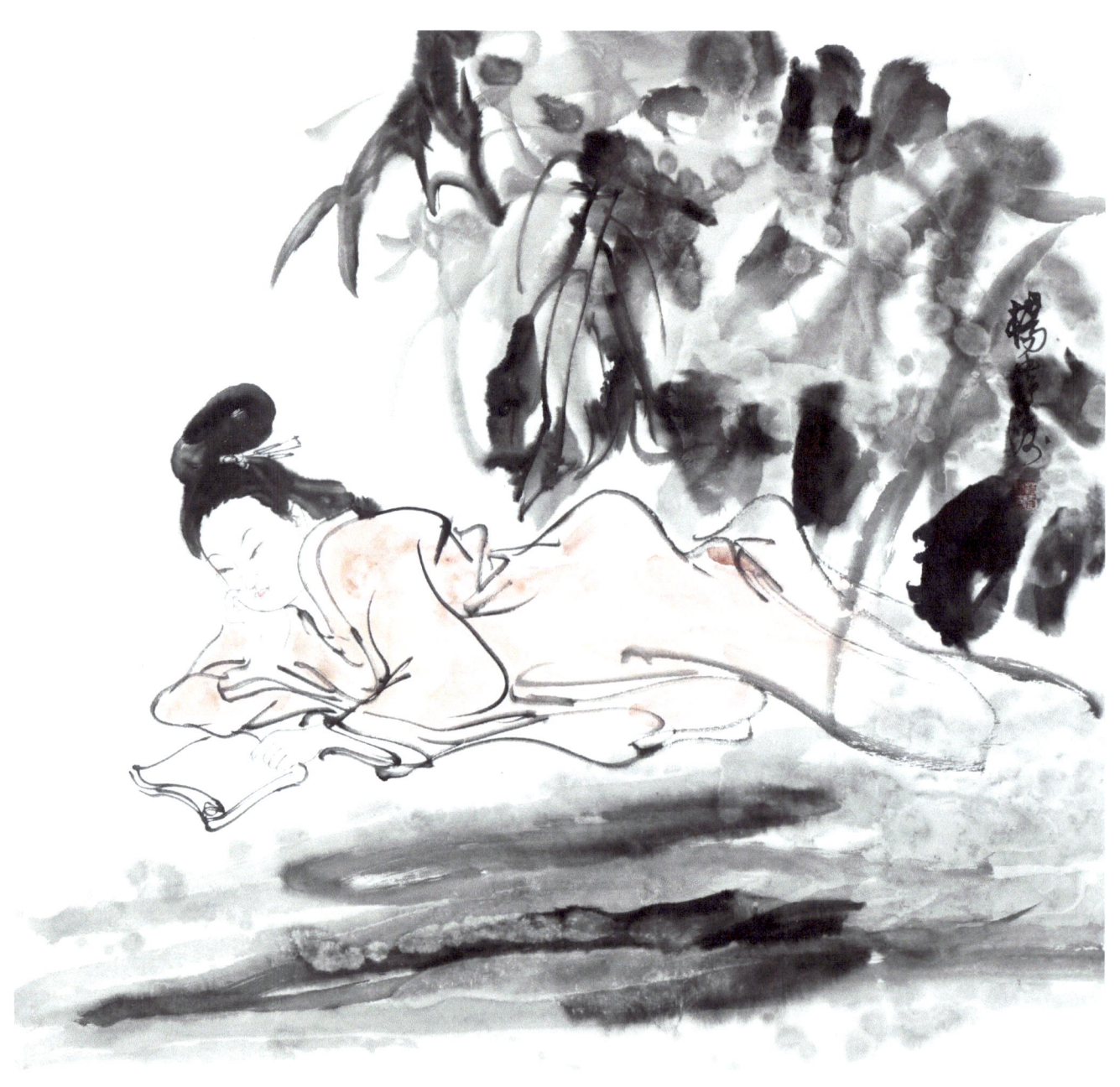

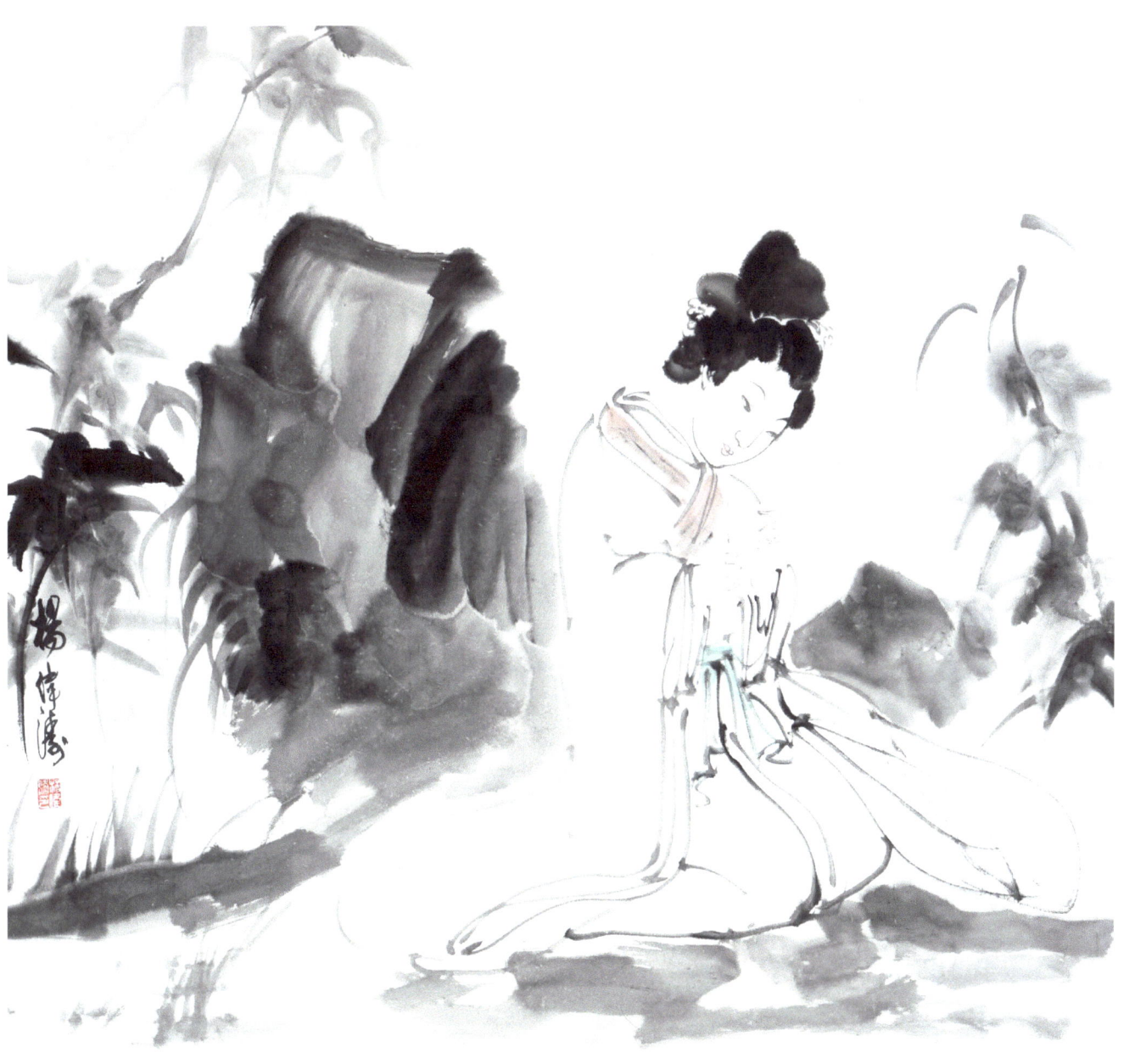

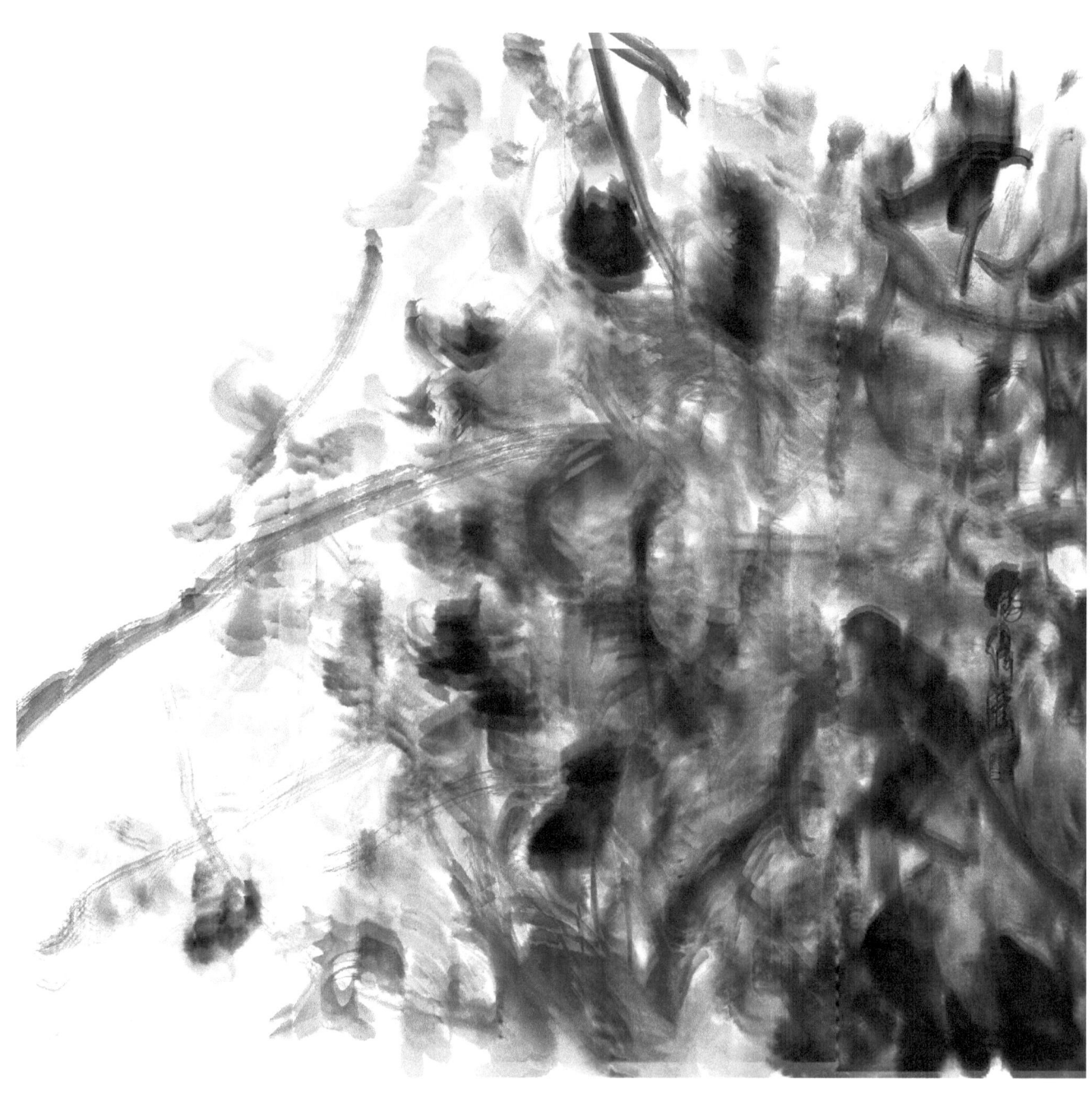

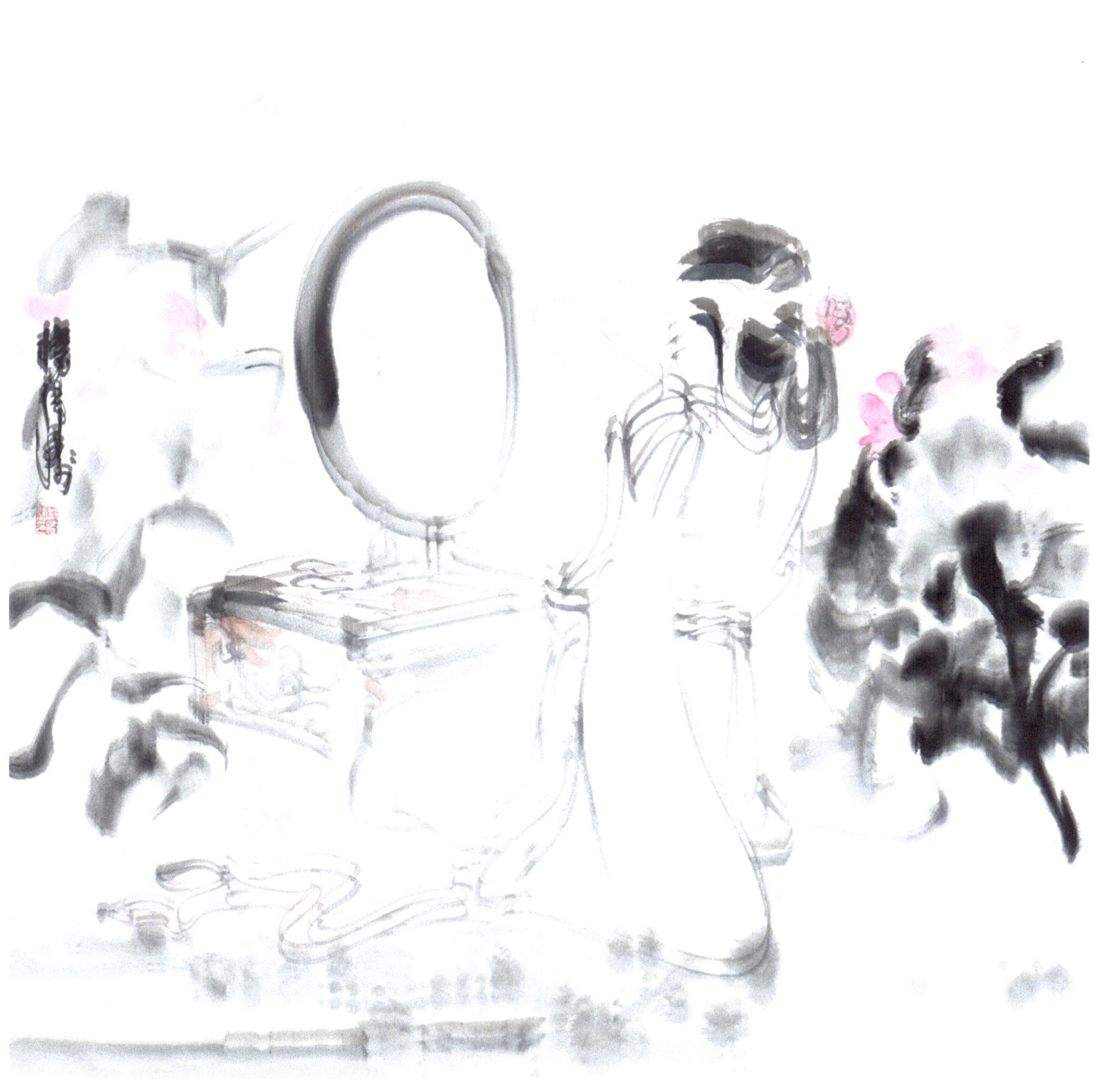

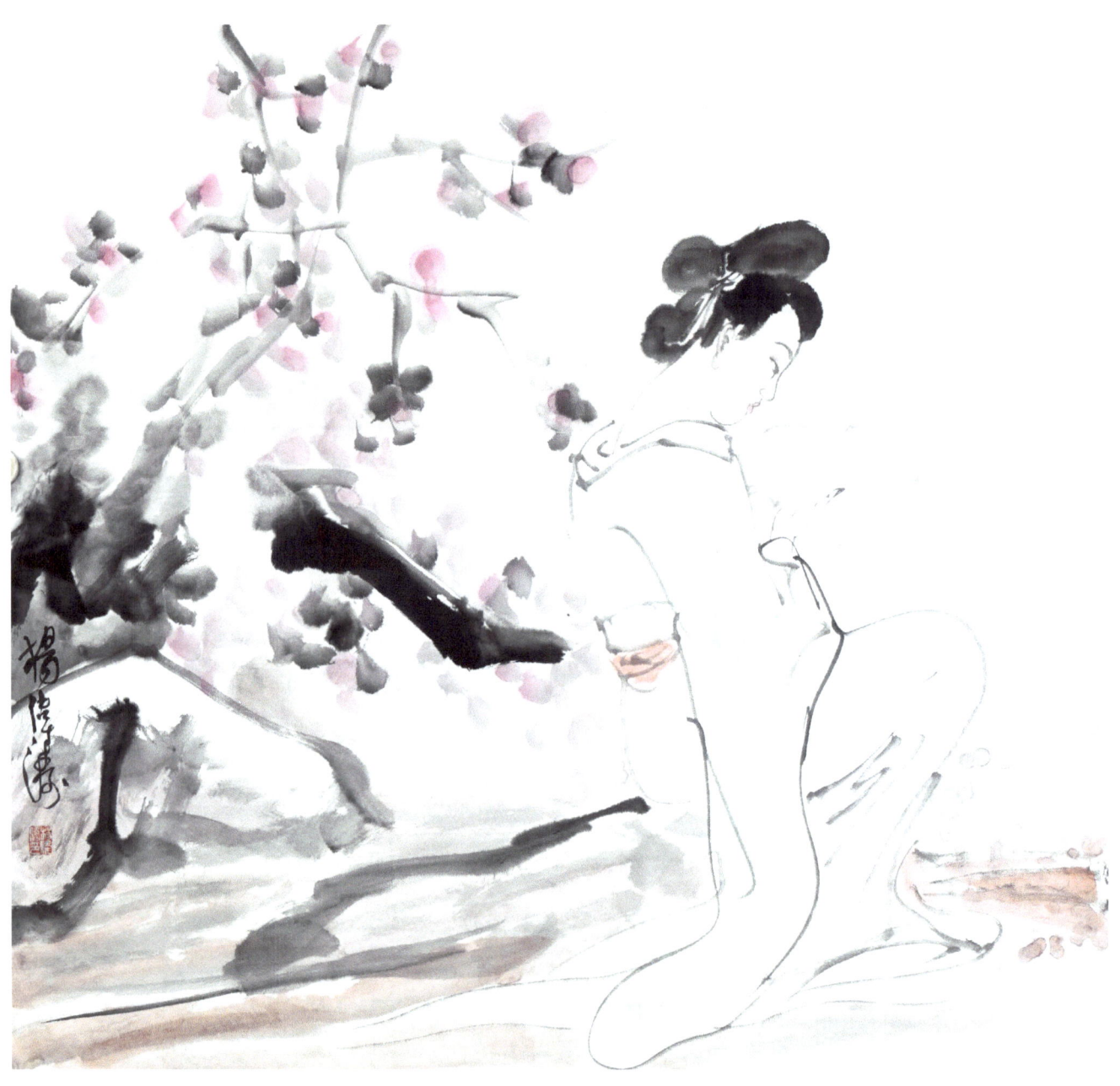

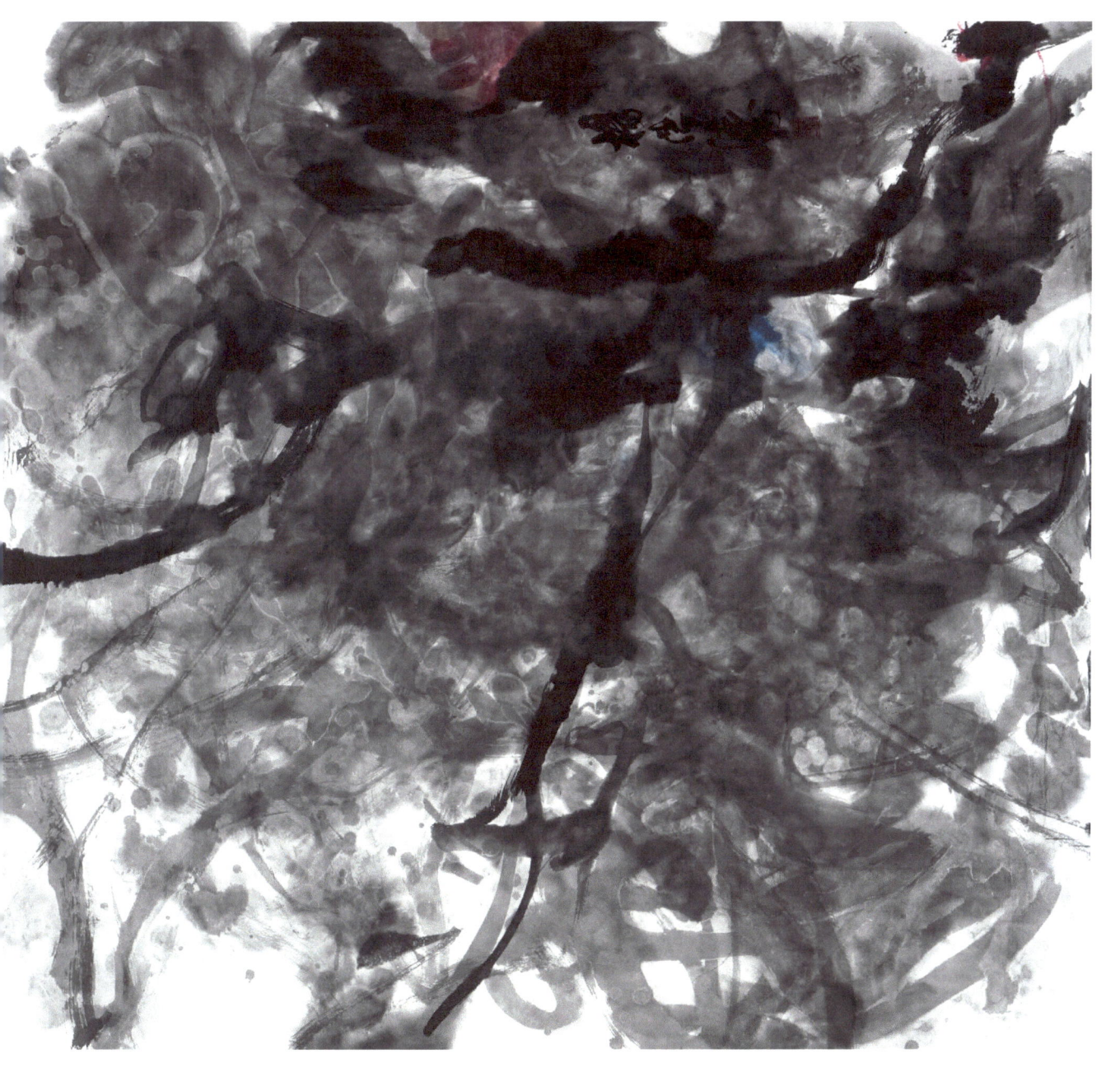

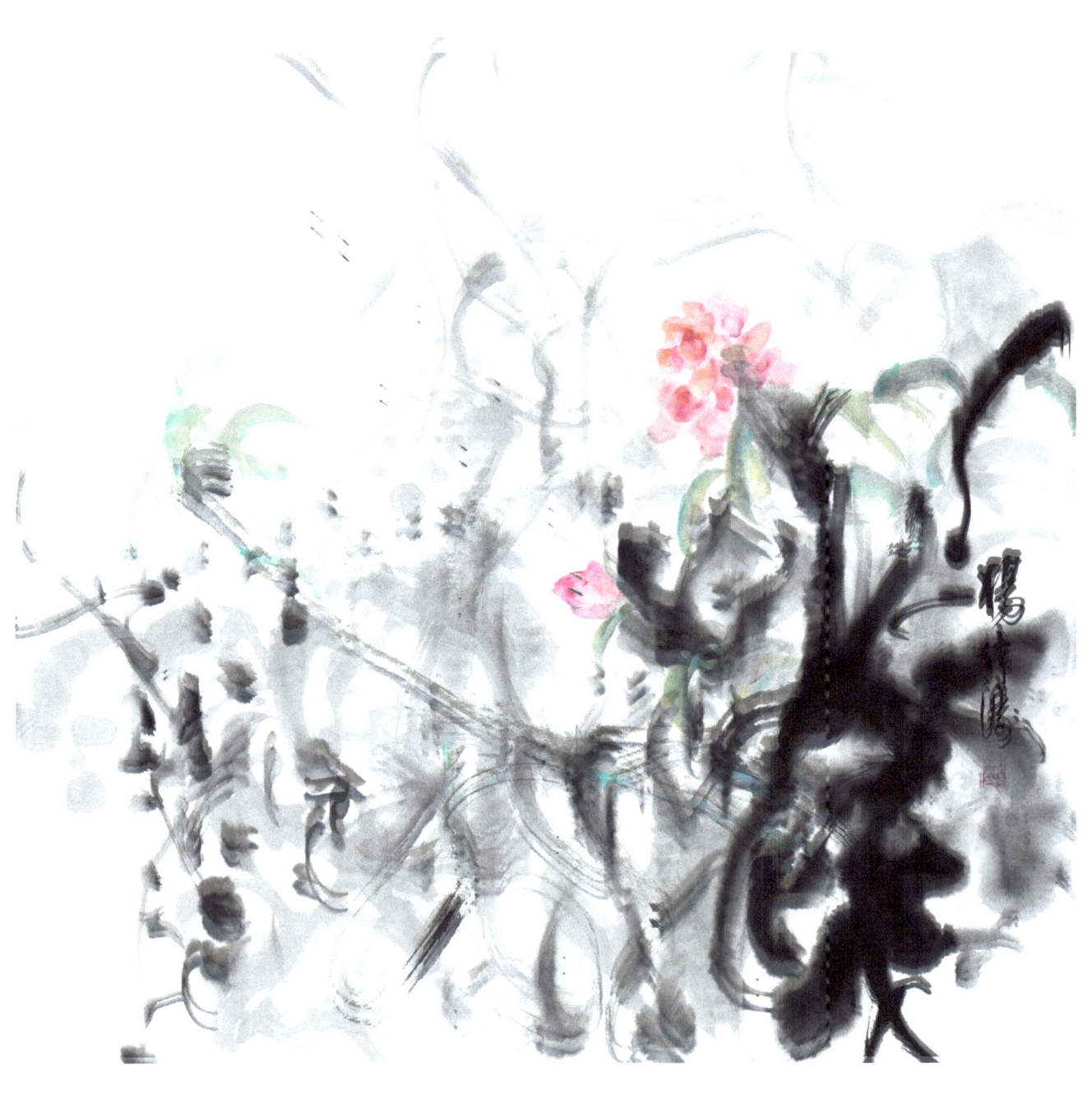

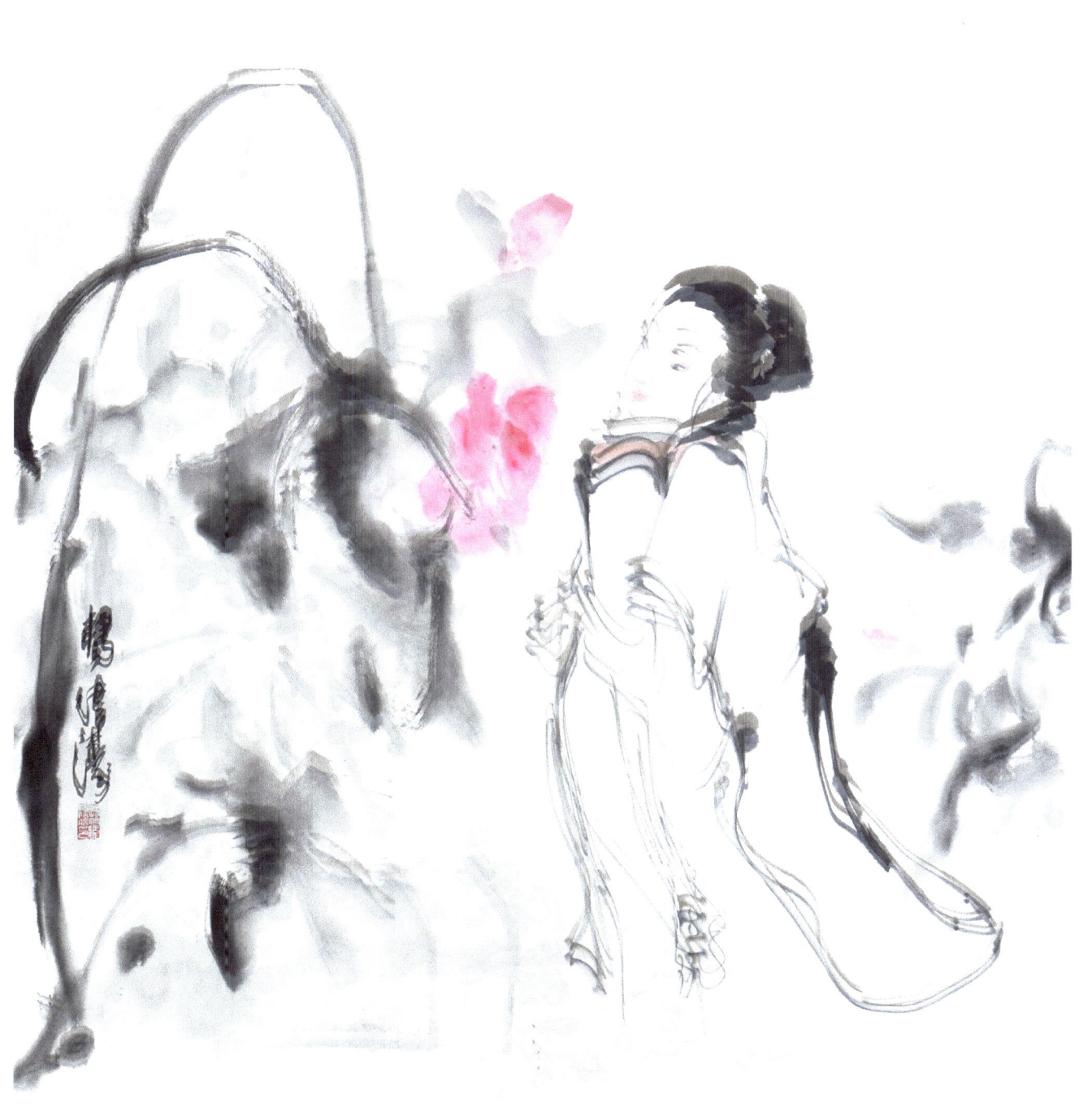

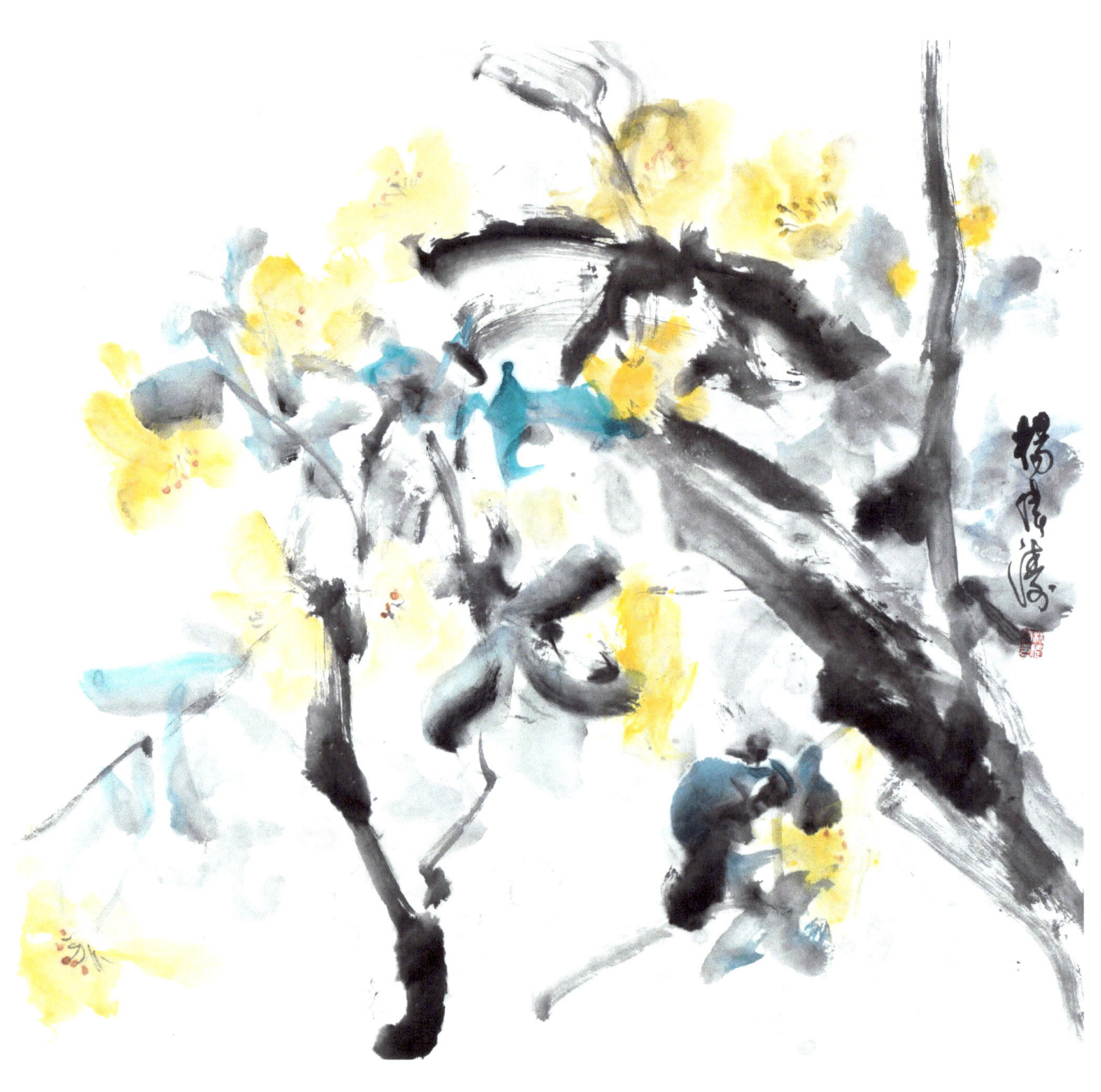

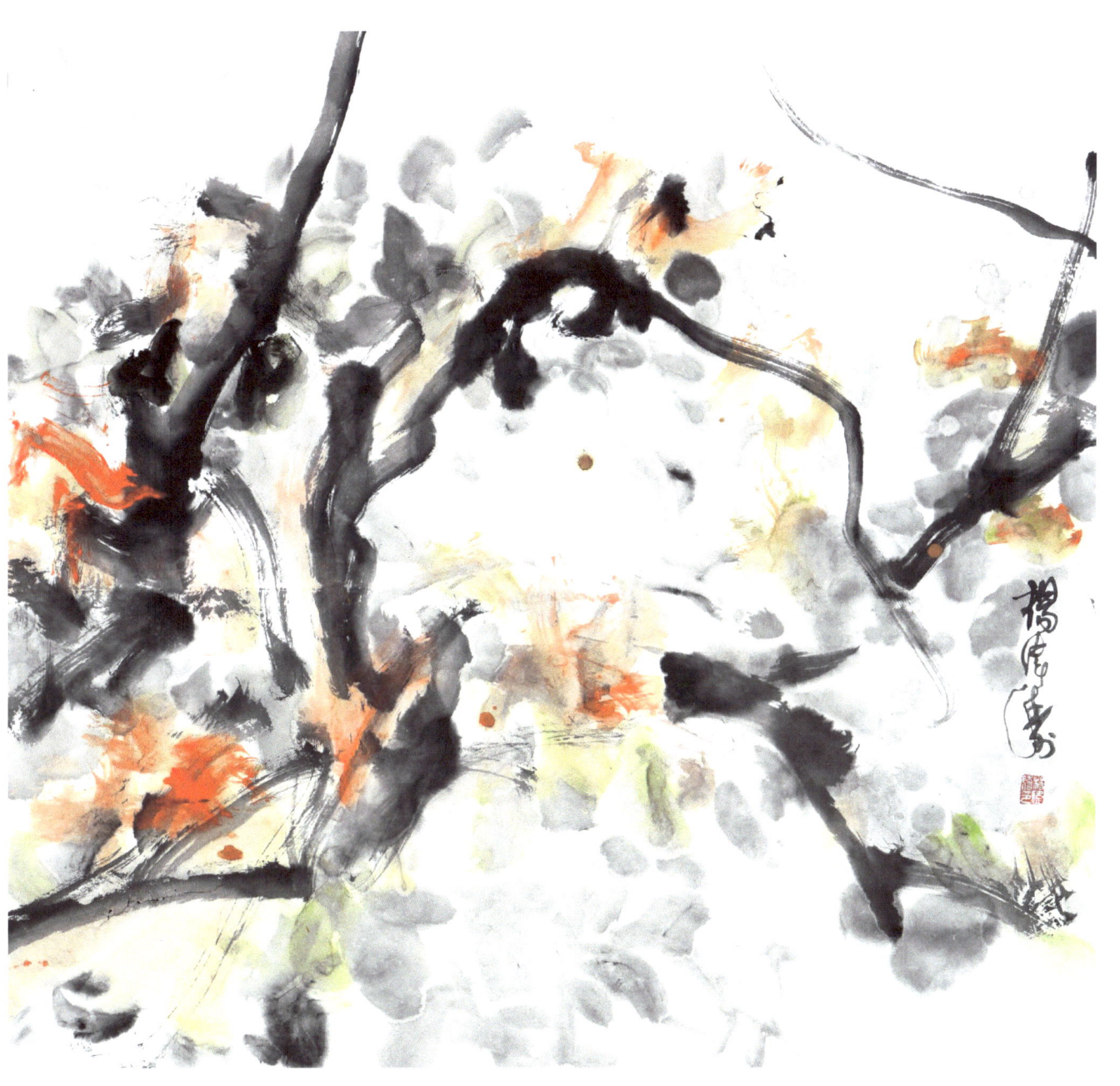

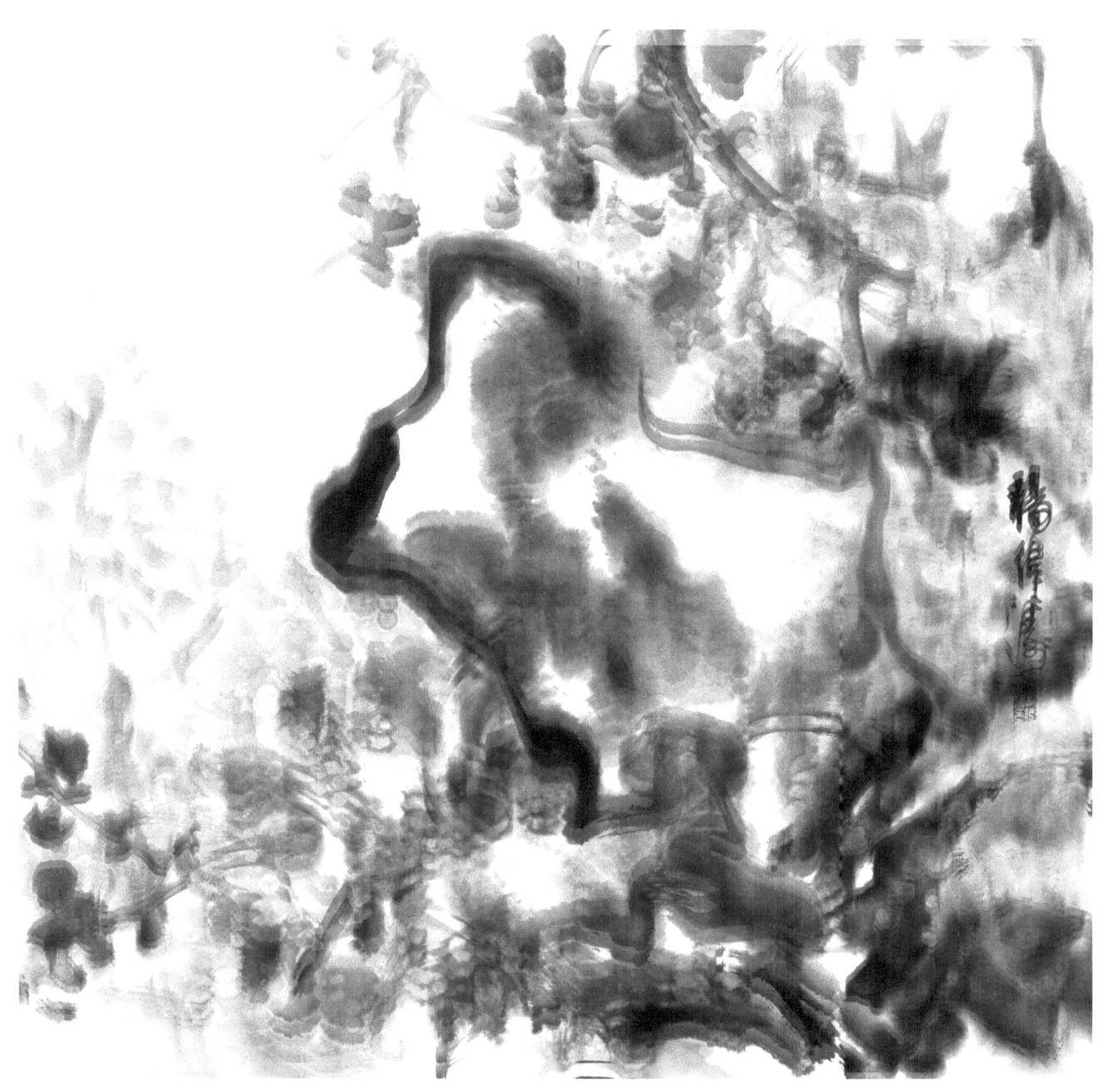

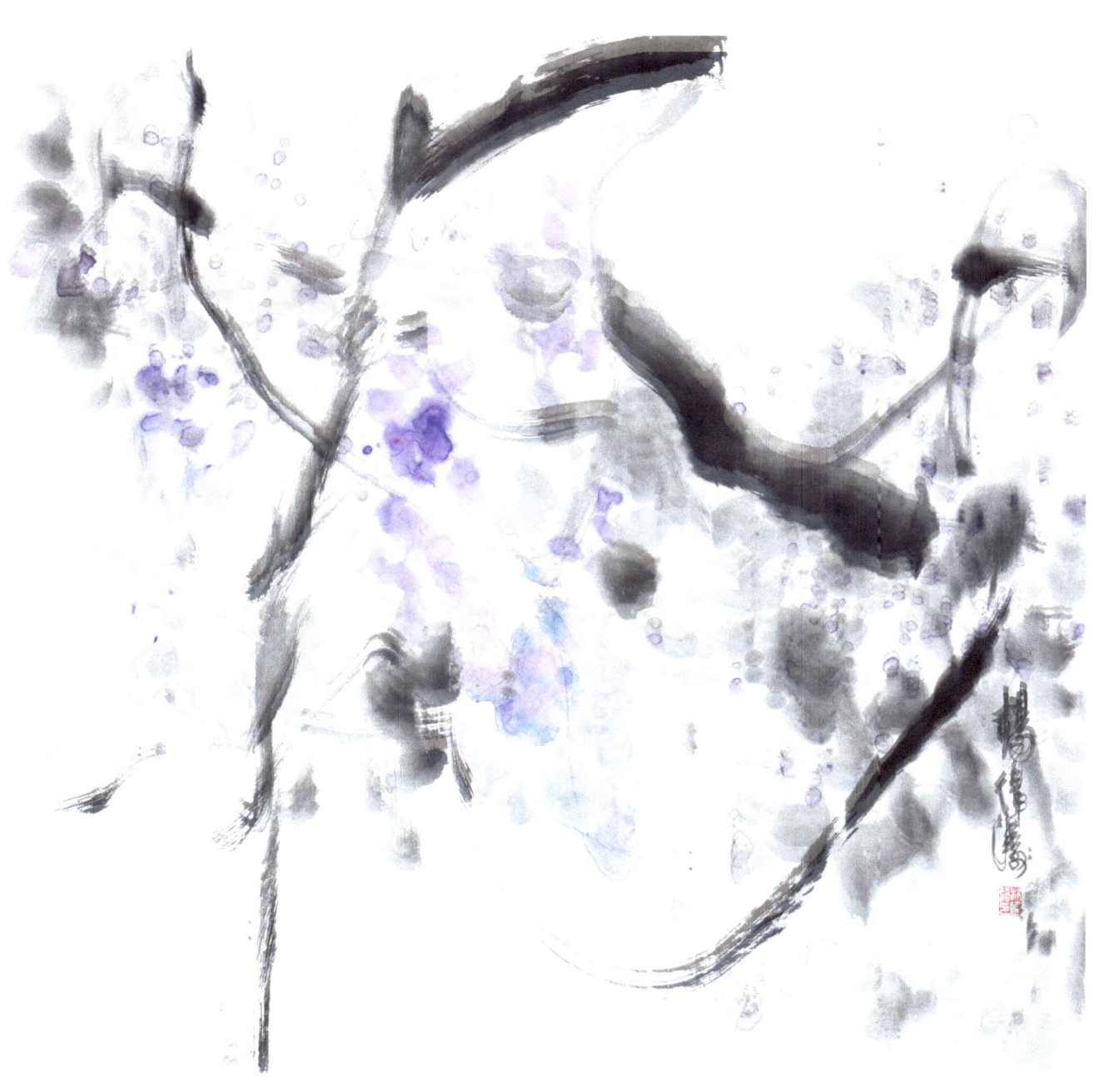

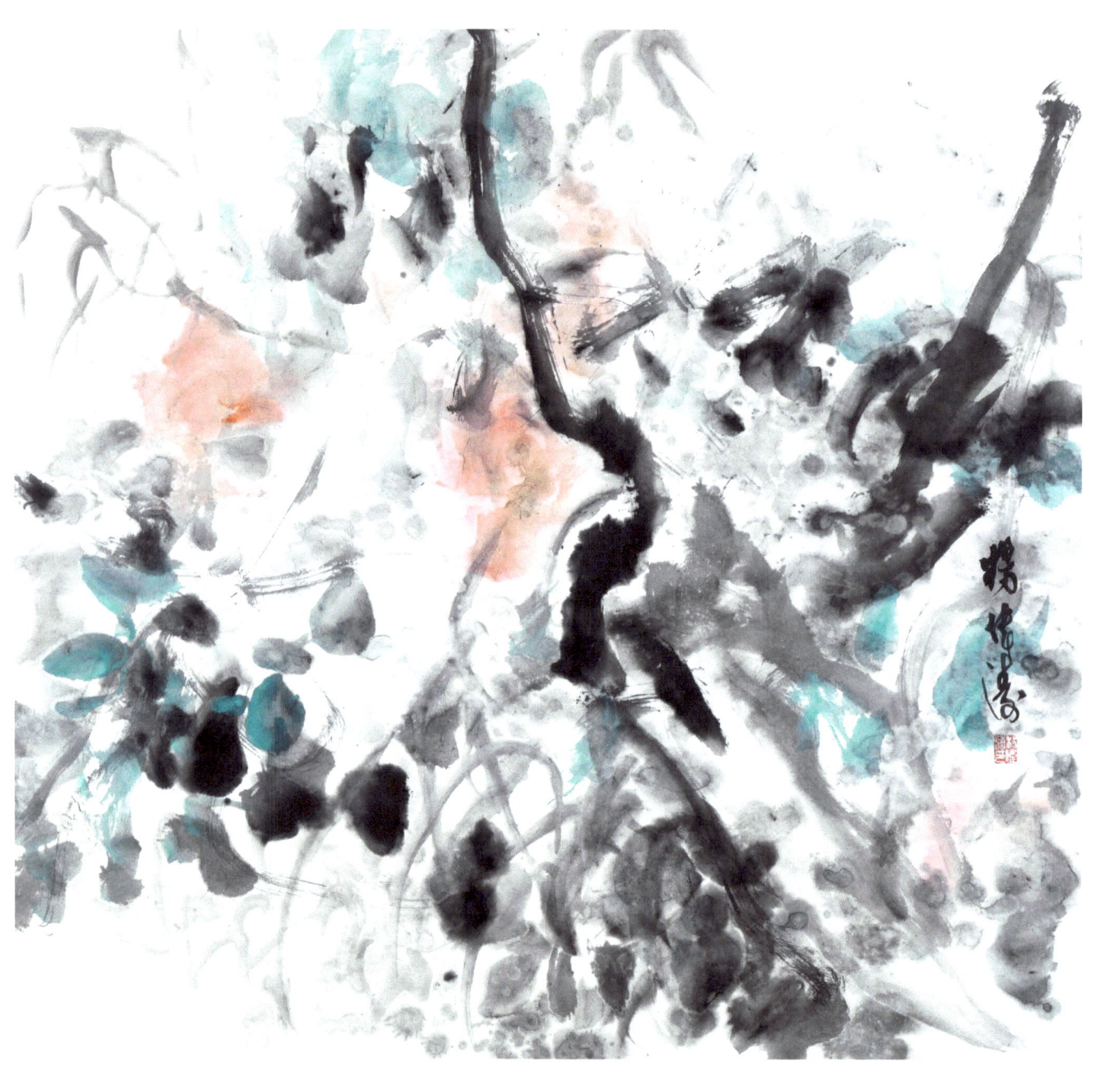

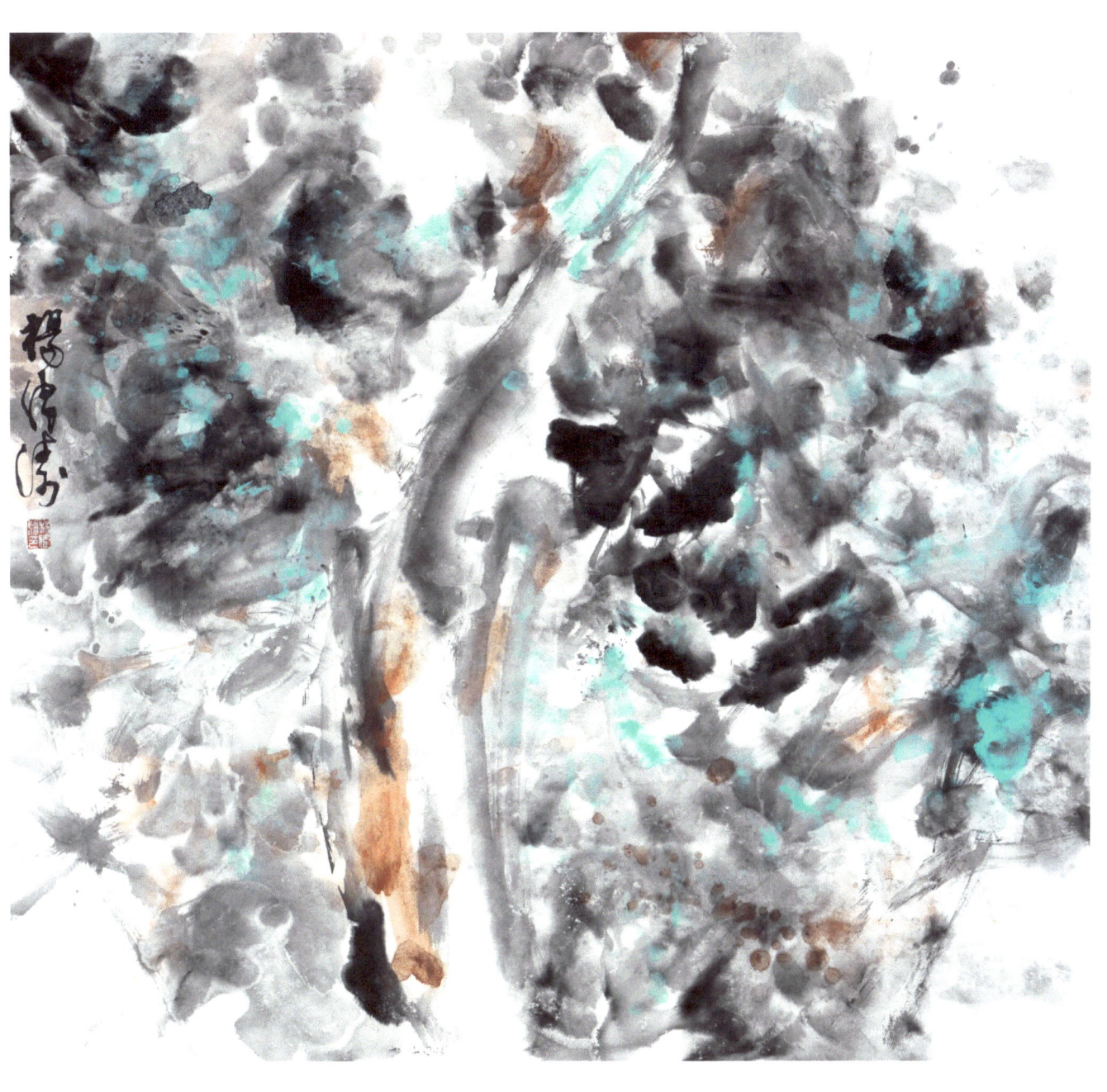